D0118771

EDGE
BOOKS

THE WORLD'S TOP TENS

THE WORLD'S MOST

DANGEROUS

STUNTS

by Tim O'Shei

Consultant:
Dr. Solomon Davidoff, Assistant Professor
General Education/Broadcasting
New England Institute of Art
Brookline, Massachusetts

Capstone
press
Mankato, Minnesota

Edge Books are published by Capstone Press,
151 Good Counsel Drive, P.O. Box 669, Mankato, Minnesota 56002.
www.capstonepress.com

Library of Congress Cataloging-in-Publication Data
O'Shei, Tim.
    The world's most dangerous stunts / by Tim O'Shei.
    p. cm.—(Edge books. The world's top tens)
    Summary: "Describes in countdown format 10 of the most dangerous stunts ever
attempted"—Provided by publisher.
    Includes bibliographical references and index.
    ISBN-13: 978-0-7368-5457-3 (hardcover)
    ISBN-10: 0-7368-5457-6 (hardcover)
    1. Daredevils—Juvenile literature. I. Title. II. World's top tens (Mankato, Minn.)
GV1469.25.D359O84 2006
791—dc22   2005019424

Editorial Credits
Angie Kaelberer, editor; Kate Opseth, set designer; Jenny Bergstrom, book designer;
    Kelly Garvin, photo researcher/photo editor

Photo Credits
AP Photo/James Knox, 8, 26 (top right); Wide World Photos, 22, 27 (bottom left)
As published in the Chicago Sun-Times, Inc. Copyright 2005. Chicago Sun-Times, Inc.
    Reprinted with permission, 18, 27 (middle left)
Aurora/Dennis Brack/IPN, 14, 27 (top left)
"BIGFOOT" is a registered trademark of BIGFOOT 4x4, Inc. 6311 N. Lindbergh
    Blvd., St. Louis, MO 63042 USA, 4
Corbis, 11, 26 (bottom left); Bettmann, 6, 7, 15, 26 (top left); Larry Kasperek/
    NewSport, 16, 27 (top right); Mike Powell, 29; Osports.cn/NewSport/NewSport,
    12, 26 (bottom right); Sygma/Celestin Roger, 25, 27 (bottom right); Vince
    Streano, cover
Getty Images Inc./Spencer Platt/Newsmakers, 24
naturepl.com/Leo & Mandy Dickinson, 20, 27 (middle right)

1 2 3 4 5 6 11 10 09 08 07 06

TABLE OF
CONTENTS

DANGEROUS STUNTS

In 1999, Dan Runge jumped the monster truck Bigfoot 14 over a jet airplane. But even that amazing stunt wasn't crazy enough to make our top 10 list.

Imagine riding a motorcycle—into the Grand Canyon. Think about what it's like to be cold—because you're frozen in a block of ice. Picture yourself on the high floors of a skyscraper—clinging to the building with suction cups.

The people in this book have done those things and more. Some people call them stunt performers. Others call them daredevils.

Many people call them crazy.

No matter what words are used to describe them, these people have guts. They have bravery. They have no fear.

More than anything, they thrive on danger.

ESCAPE ARTIST

Houdini's crate was nailed shut and lowered into the East River.

BIRTH NAME: Ehrich Weiss

BORN: March 24, 1874, in Budapest, Hungary

RAISED IN: Appleton, Wisconsin

DIED: October 31, 1926, from a burst appendix

In another famous stunt, Houdini attached a ball and chain to his legs before diving into a swimming pool.

Magician Harry Houdini was a master at breaking free from padlocks and chains. One of his most famous stunts included handcuffs, a big box, and a deep river.

On July 7, 1912, Houdini was on a large boat on New York City's East River. A huge crowd of people watched as Houdini's hands and ankles were cuffed. He was crammed into a wooden crate, which was then nailed shut and wrapped with metal bands.

Ropes slowly lowered the crate into the river. The crowd waited. Would Houdini escape? The answer came in less than one minute, when Houdini's head bobbed in the water. No one knew exactly how, but the escape artist had cheated death once again.

9

FIRST HUMAN CANNONBALL: George Loyal in 1875

EARLY CANNONS: Used rubber springs to push people out of the cannons

NEW RECORD: In 2002, David Smith Sr. broke the record again, traveling 201 feet, 4 inches (62 meters).

FYI: David Smith Sr. has never broken a bone.

HUMAN CANNONBALL

Have you ever shot a basketball high into a net? Human cannonballs work much the same way. Compressed air forces human cannonballs out of the cannon at 70 miles (113 kilometers) per hour. They reach heights of 100 feet (30 meters) as they travel in an arc and fall into a safety net.

David Smith Sr. is today's most famous human cannonball. He teamed with his son David Jr. in a double record-breaking stunt.

On May 29, 1998, both Smiths performed at Kennywood Park in Pennsylvania. They were launched into the air at the same time.

David Jr. landed first, traveling 181 feet, 1 inch (55 meters). That was enough for the record! But a moment later, David Sr. landed. His mark was 185 feet, 10 inches (57 meters), breaking the record his son had just set.

8 WING WALKER

Ormer Locklear made wing walking popular. But the first time he inched across an airplane wing, he wasn't doing it as a stunt.

In 1917, Locklear joined the U.S. Army Air Service. During a student flight one day, he couldn't see directions being given to him from the ground. Locklear left his teacher at the controls and climbed on the wing to get a better look. It wasn't meant to be a daredevil move. But the attention Locklear received convinced him to continue wing walking.

Locklear left the military in 1919 to work as a barnstormer. He did handstands on the wings and hung from the plane by a bar or rope held in his teeth. His craziest stunts involved jumping from one airplane to another, or from an airplane to a car.

Locklear died in 1920 while doing an airplane stunt for a movie called *The Skywayman*. The movie's producers left his crash and death in the movie.

During barnstormer shows, Locklear balanced on the top wing of his airplane.

LOCKLEAR'S AIRPLANE: A Curtiss JN-4D, nicknamed a "Jenny"

NICKNAME: Traveling pilots were called barnstormers because they put on shows at local farms.

7

Danny Way jumped the Great Wall's Ju Yong Guan gate.

SKATE STUNT

The Great Wall of China is earth's longest structure, winding about 4,000 miles (6,500 kilometers) through northern China. At some points, it is 30 feet (9.1 meters) wide and 25 feet (7.6 meters) tall.

Over the years, daredevils have used different vehicles to try to jump over the wall. Danny Way wanted to be the first person to jump the wall on a skateboard. He designed a 32-foot (9.8-meter) ramp to give him the speed to propel him over the wall.

July 9, 2005, was the big day. On his first try, Way made it over the wall but landed on his back instead of his board. On his next try, Way sailed 61 feet (19 meters) before landing cleanly on the other side. But Way wasn't finished yet.

During his third attempt, onlookers gasped as Way spun on his board in a complete circle in the air. He repeated the trick before putting away his board for the day.

OTHER RECORDS: Longest distance jumped, 79 feet (24 meters); height above a ramp, 23.5 feet (7.2 meters)

CRAZY TRICK: In 1997, Way dropped out of a helicopter onto a skateboard ramp; the trick is called the Bomb Drop.

6

CANYON JUMP

Idaho's Snake River Canyon is a quarter mile (0.4 kilometer) wide. Even daredevil Evel Knievel couldn't clear that gap on a regular motorcycle. Instead, he used a rocket-powered bike called a skycycle.

On September 8, 1974, Knievel strapped into the skycycle and fired up the engine. The rockets pushed the skycycle up the ramp.

But then the unexpected happened. The skycycle released its parachute before it left the ramp. As the rockets pushed the cycle up, the drag caused by the parachute pulled it down. Knievel never made it across the canyon. Instead, the parachute carried him to canyon floor, just feet from the river.

Though Knievel's jump didn't go as planned, he did survive it. That alone was amazing.

The skycycle's parachute opened too soon.

REAL NAME: Robert Craig Knievel

BORN: October 17, 1938

FIRST MAJOR STUNT: Jumped over 16 cars in 1966 at Ascot Speedway in Indio, California

WORLD RECORD: During his career, Knievel broke 35 bones, putting him into the *Guinness Book of Records*.

5 FREESTYLE FALL

Pastrana has won four gold medals in freestyle motocross at the X Games.

TRAINING: Pastrana did 45 practice skydives during the two weeks before his jump.

ON FILM: Pastrana's stunt became part of a DVD called *Global Addiction*.

FYI: Parts of the Grand Canyon are 1 mile (1.6 kilometers) deep.

At age 10, Travis Pastrana dreamed of jumping a dirt bike into the Grand Canyon with a parachute. By the time Pastrana was 18, he was a star motocross racer and freestyle competitor. He decided to make his dream come true. Filmmaker Greg Godfrey agreed to tape the stunt.

On November 14, 2001, Pastrana hopped on his motorcycle in the desert near the Grand Canyon. He gunned the bike up a ramp and rocketed into the canyon.

For about 1,000 feet (305 meters), Pastrana fell freely until he gained enough speed to open the parachute. He then pulled his parachute, jumped off the bike, and safely floated the last 500 feet (152 meters) to the canyon floor.

Pastrana did the stunt twice. For the second jump, he did a backflip and a heel clicker before releasing the bike.

Pastrana wanted to do a third jump, with two backflips. His dad talked him out of it.

4

Dan Goodwin climbed 110 stories in six hours.

Age during Sears Tower climb: 25

Other successful climb: The World Trade Center's north tower in 1983

Unsuccessful climb: In 1999, he tried to climb the World Trade Center's south tower, but police stopped him.

SCALING THE TOWER

Dan Goodwin's nickname is "Spider Dan." Like the comic character Spider-Man, Goodwin has a talent for climbing buildings.

Of course, Goodwin couldn't make his climbs without some help. Suction cups attached to his hands and feet allow him to grip glass windows and climb up the sides of buildings.

Goodwin's most famous climb was May 25, 1981. He climbed the Sears Tower, which was then the tallest building in the world. The tower is 110 floors and 1,450 feet (442 meters) high. Goodwin reached the top in six hours.

At the top, police arrested Goodwin for trespassing. Once Goodwin paid a $35 fine, he was released.

Later that year, Goodwin climbed another Chicago skyscraper, the John Hancock Center. Firefighters tried to stop him by aiming hoses at him and shooting water. It didn't work. Goodwin climbed 100 floors until he reached the top.

3 BASE JUMPING

The Great Trango Tower is in the Karakorum mountain range in Pakistan.

BASE jumping is like skydiving without an airplane. The sport gets its name from four jump sites. *B* is for buildings, *A* is for antennae or cranes, *S* is for spans or bridges, and *E* is for earth, which includes cliffs.

Nic Feteris is a BASE jumper. Glenn Singleman is a mountain climber. In 1992, the two Australians combined their talents to jump off a massive cliff in Pakistan. The cliff is called the Great Trango Tower. Its height is 19,300 feet (5,800 meters).

On August 26, 1992, Feteris and Singleman stepped off the cliff. They fell at a speed of 125 miles (202 kilometers) per hour. Both men lost control and came within a few feet of smashing into the cliff wall. A few seconds later, their parachutes opened. When they safely reached the ground, they held the world record for the tallest-ever BASE jump.

BASE INVENTOR: Carl Boenish in the late 1970s; he died during a cliff jump in 1984.

ON FILM: Singleman and Feteris filmed their jump with cameras attached to their bodies. The video is called *BASE Climb*.

FYI: BASE jumping is against the law almost everywhere.

2

Petit used a pole to balance on the wire between the World Trade Center towers.

EARLY STUNTS: Began as a juggler on the streets of Paris, France

DISTANCE BETWEEN THE TOWERS: 140 feet (43 meters)

FYI: In 2002, Petit published a book about his stunt called *To Reach the Clouds*.

HIGH-WIRE WALKER

In 1968, 18-year-old Philippe Petit read a newspaper article about a pair of towers being built in New York City. When finished, they would be 110 stories high—the tallest towers in the world.

Petit got an idea. He wanted to walk on a high wire between the towers, which were part of the World Trade Center. He began learning how to wire walk.

During the night of August 6, 1974, three friends helped Petit stretch a wire between the towers. About 7:00 the next morning, Petit stepped onto the wire and began walking.

A crowd of about 100,000 people gathered below. People gasped as Petit began doing dance steps 1,350 feet (410 meters) above them.

Forty-five minutes after he started, Petit got off the wire. His stunt was illegal, but he didn't get in trouble. In fact, he was asked to autograph a steel beam at the top of one of the towers.

ICE MAN

In November 2002, David Blaine stepped between two huge chunks of ice. The chunks were then joined together, with Blaine on the inside. In the middle of Times Square in New York City, Blaine was frozen inside of an ice cube the size of a van.

Blaine wore only a cap, boots, and pants. A special gel kept his skin from getting too cold. Tubes inserted into the ice brought him water and oxygen. A tube connected to his body allowed Blaine to urinate.

Medics stood nearby, watching Blaine's heart monitor. If Blaine's body stopped working properly, they were ready to cut into the ice and pull him out. Amazingly, that didn't happen. Blaine survived 61 icy hours. The feat was featured in a TV show called *David Blaine: Frozen in Time*.

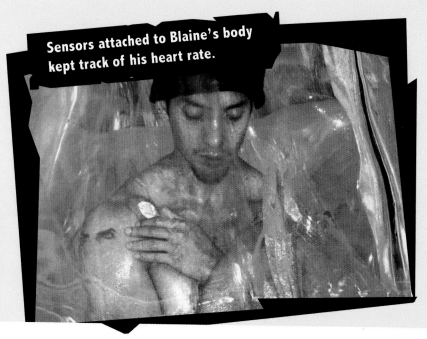

Sensors attached to Blaine's body kept track of his heart rate.

BIRTH NAME: David Blaine White

FIRST PERFORMANCES: Did card tricks on New York City streets in the 1990s

HERO: Harry Houdini

FYI: In 2003, Blaine lived 44 days without food in a transparent box 30 feet (9.1 meters) above London, England.

The World's Most DANGEROUS STUNTS

10

ESCAPE ARTIST

9

HUMAN CANNONBALL

WING WALKER

7

8

SKATE STUNT

CANYON JUMP

6

FREESTYLE FALL

5

SCALING THE TOWER

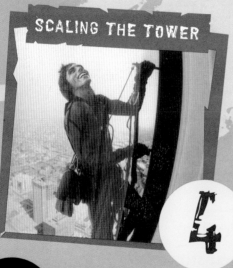

3

4

BASE JUMPING

ICE MAN

1

2

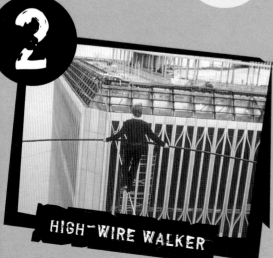

HIGH-WIRE WALKER

UNDERSTANDING STUNTS

For people who do stunts, life is a roller coaster. The steeper it climbs and the faster it travels, the more they like it.

Deep water. Big jumps. Tight places. Bone-chilling cold. Nail-biting altitude.

Most people are satisfied to see these things in pictures and movies. But daredevils don't want to just see them. Daredevils want to experience all of these things and more. That's what makes them different from most people.

But no one becomes a daredevil overnight. Thrillseekers plan their stunts carefully and practice for them for months or even years before attempting them. To do otherwise is to risk injury or death. These crazy stunts are best left to the pros!

Daredevils love the excitement of extreme stunts, like bungee jumping over a rushing river.

GLOSSARY

altitude (AL-ti-tood)—the height of an object above the ground

barnstormer (BAHRN-storm-ur)—a pilot who traveled from place to place doing airplane stunts

canyon (KAN-yuhn)—a deep valley with steep sides; a river wears away rocky land to form a canyon.

oxygen (OK-suh-juhn)—a colorless gas in the air that people and animals need to breathe

parachute (PA-ruh-shoot)—a large piece of strong, lightweight fabric; parachutes allow people to jump from high places and float safely to the ground.

skyscraper (SKYE-skray-pur)—a very tall building

trespass (TRESS-pass)—to enter a building or other area without permission

READ MORE

Cobb, Vicki. *Harry Houdini.* DK Biography. New York: DK, 2005.

Hopkins, Ellen. *Air Devils: Sky Racers, Sky Divers, and Stunt Pilots.* Cover-to-Cover Books. Logan, Iowa: Perfection Learning, 2000.

Sievert, Terri. *Travis Pastrana: Motocross Legend.* Edge Books: Dirt Bikes. Mankato, Minn.: Capstone Press, 2006.

INTERNET SITES

FactHound offers a safe, fun way to find Internet sites related to this book. All of the sites on FactHound have been researched by our staff.

Here's how:

1. Visit *www.facthound.com*
2. Type in this special code **0736854576** for age-appropriate sites. Or enter a search word related to this book for a more general search.
3. Click on the **Fetch It** button.

FactHound will fetch the best sites for you!

Index